Knowing People by the Spirit

by

Roberts Liardon

Unless otherwise indicated, all Scripture quotations are taken from the *King James Version* of the Bible.

Some quotations are taken from the *New King James Version* of the Bible. Copyright © 1979, 1980, 1982, by Thomas Nelson Inc., publishers.

1st Printing

Knowing People by the Spirit
ISBN 1-890900-07-9

Copyright © 1999 by Roberts Liardon Ministries.
P.O. Box 30710
Laguna Hills, CA 92654

Published by Embassy Publishing Co.
P.O. Box 3500
Laguna Hills, CA 92654

Contents

1

Life In The Spirit

There is therefore now no condemnation to them which are in Christ Jesus, who walk not after the flesh, but after the Spirit.

Romans 8:1 (NKJ)

You can be born again and still live under condemnation. Many Christians do. But notice the rest of our text says, *"to them which walk not after the flesh, but after the Spirit."*

We often quote the first part of the verse — *"There is therefore now no condemnation to them which are in Christ Jesus,"* and end it there, but the verse does continue. We need to examine this last portion, because Christians will continually suffer from a sense of condemnation if they don't learn to live in the realm of the Spirit.

Living in the Spirit realm is really very simple. Like Kathryn Kuhlman would say, it's so easy, most people miss it. The Gospel is so simple, it takes man to mess it up.

Walking In The Spirit Is A Decision

Life in the Spirit is a decision. It's not just a feeling or a vision that comes, or something dramatic that happens to you, even though supernatural experiences may happen in your life and ministry. It's a decision about where and how you're going to live your life.

There are times when you are making decisions, or you're being hit by the enemy, that you may fluctuate a little in the realm of the Spirit, but you never have to come out of that arena.

We cannot engage in spiritual warfare unless we live in the Spirit. If we attempt warfare in the strength of our flesh, we'll get worn out. Spiritual warfare should not wear you out; it should make you stronger and more alive.

We've got to learn how to pray through the leading and unction of the Holy Spirit, and not by the flesh. It's got to be by the Spirit, in the Spirit and for the purposes of the Holy Spirit.

In the Sermon on the Mount, Jesus said, *"Blessed are they which do hunger and thirst after righteousness; for they shall be filled"* (Matthew 5:6). If there is no hunger in you, there will be no filling inside of you.

Becoming Addicted To Heaven

You have to become addicted to heaven and to the things of God! Alcoholics drink and drink until their bodies acquire a taste, and eventually a craving, for alcohol. That's the way we need to be concerning the realm of the Spirit of God. We need to keep putting the things of the Gospel and the move of the Holy Spirit in us to where we can't live without them in our life and ministry.

Some people only like to have Heaven about once a month. The rest of the time, they say, *"Let me do my thing the way I want to do it."* If you're doing this — if you're running your life and ministry according to the flesh —you'll eventually wear yourself out. If you learn to run your life and ministry by the flow of the Holy Spirit, you won't get so tired. You'll have new strength.

Walk After The Spirit

The Bible tells us to walk after the Spirit. How do you walk *"after"* something? You make a decision to go after it. Life in the Spirit is a choice to go after the things of God all the way, allowing nothing to hinder or distract you.

You've got to want the move of the Spirit in your churches bad enough to go after it. You cannot settle for soulish activity. There are sermons that are preached by the soul and there are sermons that are preached by the Spirit. You must make it your goal to preach by the unction of the Holy Spirit.

There are songs sung in the natural and songs sung in the Spirit. Go after those that come by the Spirit. Reach out for them. If you don't quite make it the first time, get back up and try again, just like a child learning to ride a bicycle. Don't give up, because if you keep hungering and thirsting, you'll get it.

A Holy Dissatisfaction

Never become satisfied with where you are in God. Become a person who has to have more, more, more! It's a part of your addiction: you're never satisfied with what you've got.

I crave Heaven! I crave the move of the Holy Spirit! I'm not happy if all I preach is just a pleasant sermon. I have to feel the unction, the anointing. I have to know that what I did was right according to Heaven.

We need to be delivered from preaching through human ability. Yes, God will use our natural abilities, and that's fine, but we shouldn't depend on them. Our dependency must be upon the Holy Spirit.

One of the greatest truths that comes out of the life of Kathryn Kuhlman, when you listen to her tapes or read her books is her total dependence upon the Holy Spirit. She expressed it constantly, stating on all the stages she preached on, *"I'm so dependent upon the Holy Spirit!"*

We must become dependent upon the Holy Spirit too. We must get to the place where we don't know how to function without the anointing of the Holy Spirit. The problem is, we have learned the art of ministry without the moving of the Holy Spirit.

We've come to the point where there's a whole generation that does not know the flow of the Holy Spirit! When the flow of the Holy Spirit comes and begins to work and manifest among them, they become nervous. They say, *"We never saw it on this fashion before"*— and they say it in a negative way, with no excitement.

We ministers must preach sermons to our people about the moving and the manifestation of the Holy Spirit — so they will not be afraid of what they will see happening in front of them in the days to come.

Becoming Normal In Heaven's Eyes

I thank God I had my roots in the Pentecostal movement. We had more Pentecost in my home than we did in our church. We had more prayer, more shouting, more praying for the sick and casting out devils in our front room than I saw in many church services.

Neighbors would come over for prayer. Even though they were sinners, they knew where to come when their children were sick. When someone faced a divorce or some other problem, guess who they would call? My mother and my grandmother. And what did we do? We prayed until we got the answer!

Often I'd come home from school and people would be laying on the front room floor. This was normal for my family, so when I began my ministry, I thought, *"Everyone does this."* I didn't know that we were such a rare breed in the earth.

We've got to know what's normal according to heaven — not what's normal according to the soulish or natural realm. The standard of what is normal to heaven is what we should crave and conform to.

Walking in the Spirit is becoming like Jesus. Walking in the Spirit is not always yielding to the natural desires of the flesh; it is staying in that high realm, on that narrow road. But you've got to make a choice to stay there.

2

Knowing People By The Spirit

In Corinthians 5:16 we read: *"Henceforth know we no man after the flesh."* If we don't know people after the flesh, then how do we know them? We've got to know them by the Holy Spirit. This is a big problem in the church today, especially among ministries, because you can view people according to what you see in the natural, but that view will not always bring accurate discernment. That view may not provide the true facts about that person.

When I was a little boy growing up in church, we'd have great people come to preach, and I'd think, *"Boy, if I could just get to meet them and shake their hand and talk with them, I'd be close to Heaven!"*

Years passed and my ministry grew to where I was able to meet some of them. I remember one case where I was behind the scenes in a meeting, and this great man came. I was so excited about meeting him.

We went out to eat. Then he did something that burst my bubble. I thought, "I can't believe he did that! He needs to go pray." What he did wasn't sin, and it wasn't wrong, but it blew my image of him. I had to go pray and get myself back together again.

The Lord took me to this verse. He said, "You can't know people after the flesh. You have to know them after the Spirit." He asked, "Do you still believe that man is anointed?"

I said, "Well, I never doubted it. I think he's one of the greatest men in the world. I've read his books. I've given to his ministry. I'll always give to his ministry."

"Then what is your problem?"

"Lord, I know what he did wasn't wrong, but my bubble burst. I need some help to get myself back together."

"Has he helped you?"

"He's helped me a lot."

"Then what's your problem?"

"Well, I don't know — but my bubble burst! Heal me. Do whatever You need to do."

"You were shocked when you saw him in the natural," the Lord responded, "What he was doing in the natural was different from the way you had seen him act before. He wasn't wrong, but he wasn't under the anointing then. You had only known him by the anointing, and when you saw him in the natural, you couldn't handle it. It short-circuited you. You're going to have to learn how to stay hooked up with people by the Spirit of God, and not allow the natural to affect you."

Watch Out For Spiritual Disconnections

Many people disconnect from ministries because they get close enough to see that the man of God puts his shoes on like everyone else; he's still human. When they see the human side of him, it short-circuits them. They don't know how to handle it.

This is a revelation we all need to come to; we're all human but anointed by God. We all have weaknesses. And when you get close enough to someone, you're going to see signs of those weaknesses. What you need to do is say, "This person is still anointed, they're still called of God; thus, I will not disconnect from them. I will pray for them and I will bless them."

This is something we have to learn right now in the Body of Christ. In the new millennium there will be many opportunities for people to disconnect from what God is doing and from those whom God is using in the earth.

This is why we must learn how to discern people by the Spirit. When people walk up to me and say certain things, I never immediately disregard them. I don't care what they look like — and some of them look very dramatic! Their hair may be sticking out in all directions, and they may be wearing bizarre clothing that looks like it came from the 1930s. But you have to go beyond that and see them with the eye of the Spirit.

If you study some of the people whom God has used mightily in the past, you won't be so quick to cut people off. That person may be the next great man or woman of God. Some of the greatest ministers in history had the most bizarre backgrounds.

So look at people by the Spirit of God and become open to what the Spirit has to say about them. You may see all kinds of things, and you may hear all kinds of things about them in the natural, but what do you know by the Spirit of God down in your inner man? Be led by the Spirit, not by your suspicions.

You can know a ministry by the Spirit. You can know a situation by the Spirit. Be careful that the words or the opinions of men do not become stronger than the Word of the Lord or what you sense by the Spirit.

Discerning A False Report

I was invited to preach at a church one time when somebody called me and said, "Do you know what kind of church you're about to go to?"

"As far as I know it's a good church." I said.

"Well, Brother Roberts, let me give you the scoop."

They proceeded to list a host of problems.

After this person deposited his beguiling report, there began to arise in me a negative feeling toward this church. I knew I had to go pray.

"Father, I thought you told me to go to this church. What about these reports I've heard?"

"I didn't give you that negative report," He said, "I told you to go." So I went.

When I got there and began to preach, I was looking around to see if what was said was true. But by the Spirit, I couldn't find anything wrong at all. In fact, we had a great meeting. People were saved, we had a good prayer line and we had a lot of fun casting out devils; it was wonderful.

After the meeting I called this person back.

"Brother," I said, "you've either been offended, or you've been misinformed. Either you're mad or you're jealous. You need to deal with it."

He got angry and never talked to me again.

I'm sharing these things with you because as we move into the new millennium, God is going to begin to do some unusual things. Ministries unlike any we have seen before will come on the scene in a very bold manner. We must be sensitive to them by the Spirit of God. If we are not, we may disconnect ourselves from a relationship or from a ministry gift that could help us accomplish what we're called to do.

3

Holding On To Divine Relationships

You must have enough humility to receive from people you may not like in the natural. Knowing someone by the Spirit will enable you to have a great time with them, even though you may have nothing in common with them in the natural. That doesn't mean you abort your association with them, it means you hold onto your connection with them in the Spirit.

You will have many opportunities to lose your divine connections and appointments, but it is these very relationships that will help you develop the kind of character you need to succeed in life and ministry.

Great ministers don't fall because of their anointings; they fall because they did not allow God to build strong character in them. Part of building strong character is having people around you who can see your blind spots and speak into them. We all have areas we can't see, and those are usually where the devil gains his entrance and infects other aspects of life, leading to a downfall.

There are people who believed in my ministry when I had no ministry. They prayed for something that no one else saw. You must hold fast to relationships like that. They are your spiritual founders. Don't lose them because they are the ones who believed in you when you were nothing. They are the kinds of people that will look beyond your prestige and success and say things that will help you as a person.

A Divine Relationship Aborted

Let me give you an illustration of this from history. When John Alexander Dowie came from Australia to California, Maria Woodworth Etter was traveling as a pioneer Pentecostal preacher. "Mother Etter," as they called her, spoke in tongues and had the nine gifts of the Spirit even before the great Azusa Street outpouring.

When Dowie came to California, he began to hold meetings in a hotel room, and people started to get healed. His fame grew quickly here in America. At about this time, he heard reports of a little woman named Etter who was anointed of God to preach and perform miracles. Back then, women preachers didn't have much of a voice. But Mother Etter was strong and unique in everything that she did;

she was a real pioneer. It was unusual for a woman Pentecostal preacher to have a 12,000 seat tent and travel around the country; she had to be anointed to make it.

In her meetings people would fall into trances. This generation doesn't know much about trances, but in her day it was normal. Sinners and saints would fall into a trance and their physical man would freeze, while their spirit would be out moving with God in the realm of the spirit. God would give them a vision of Heaven or Hell, or take them some place and show them something. It happened in the Bible and it may happen again in your ministries at times. (Acts 10:10) When someone falls into a trance, don't get nervous, just act normal, because it is normal.

Heated Confrontations

So Dowie went to one of Mother Etter's meetings and sat in the back watching all the things that were happening. People were falling out, wailing and crying while she was upon the stage doing her thing. Dowie just couldn't handle it. Afterwards, Dowie began to blast Etter from his pulpit. He accused her of operating under the influence of familiar spirits. When Mrs. Etter heard about Dowie's comments, she confronted him face to face.

"You had better quit making fun of my meetings because what is happening is of the Holy Ghost," she warned.

Dowie responded, "Well I don't believe in all that falling down, or in those trances. I think it's a bunch of emotionalism."

"I don't allow emotionalism in my meetings and I guard against fanaticism," Mrs. Etter responded, "but I will allow the Holy Spirit to operate in my meetings."

Dowie and Etter never became friends. One reason Dowie made the mistakes he made later in life, if you look at it from a historical perspective, was because their relationship had been aborted. Six or seven years before Dowie died, he made some very negative declarations. He thought he was Elijah and he built a city that God never called him to build. Jesus never said, "Go ye and build me cities." He said, *"Go into all the world and preach the gospel to every creature."* (Mark 16:15) Dowie built a city because he was tired of overcoming the opposition that Chicago gave him. He was trying to do something to counteract the persecution, as well as to help his ego.

The only person I know about in history, that could look Dowie in the eyes and say, "Dowie, you're making a mistake," was Mrs. Etter. I believe God had arranged for them to meet by divine appointment at that time in California so that they could have a spiritual relationship that would benefit the both of them.

Mrs. Etter could have learned how to have stronger meetings through Dowie, because he packed them in by the thousands. They could have learned a lot from each other. But the devil saw fit to cause discord in their very first meeting and split them.

The only person I know that could have spoke beyond Dowie's anointing, fame and strength, was Mrs. Etter. Those around Dowie did not have the strength or position in the realm of the spirit to speak into him. You have to have a ranking in the spirit to speak to some of these people. She had that ranking, she had that position, she had that anointing, she had that development of the Spirit to understand things beyond the natural. She could have said to Dowie, you're making a mistake here. But Dowie said, "She will never preach in my city." Well, after he died, she preached there. But they missed the relationship, they missed the connection because they could not overcome the natural and know each other by the Spirit.

4

Developing Spiritual Accountability

Part of building strong character is maintaining relationships with people who can see your blind spots. You have to acknowledge when someone is speaking by the Spirit and then let their words begin to work inside you.

There have been things said to me that my flesh didn't like. I had to make my flesh walk in the fruits of the Spirit because it wanted to walk in anger. My emotions were saying, no, no, no, while something deep inside was saying, yes, yes, yes! That's right! Receive it!

These are the times you want to walk away from these people and never speak to them again for the rest of your life!

In order to know people by the spirit, you must learn to listen to people by the Spirit. You have to know when God is trying to speak to you through them. They might not even know it, but an inner witness from God will stir within you. This is part of being led by the Spirit.

Living Out Of The Inner Man

In Romans 8:14, Paul writes: *For as many as are led by the Spirit of God, they are the sons of God.*

If you are truly led by the Spirit, you'll be open to hear what He has to say to you, no matter who it comes through. This is part of spiritual accountability. You need people around you who can speak into your life by the Spirit and help you develop a strong inner man. You can't live by the anointing, my friend. You have to live out of the strength of your inner man.

I wish I could get ministers to understand this!

Samson and Joseph both carried great anointings, but Joseph survived and Samson did not. Joseph survived because he lived from the strength of his inner man. When Potiphar's wife said, "Come and sleep with me," Joseph replied, "I will not," and he ran from her. Samson, on the other hand, offered no inner resistance. When Delilah began to seduce him, he surrendered immediately and it led to his downfall. Both were anointed men of God, but Joseph had allowed the dealings of God to develop inner character in him.

God's Call Is Without Repentance

The gifts and call are irrevocable; God will never take them back. Dowie still carried an anointing to heal the sick during the last few years of his life when he thought he was Elijah. It's amazing how the anointing sticks with people. That anointing sticks and sticks and sticks. When you've got it, my brother and sister, you've got it! Although it may wane or go dormant because of what you do in the natural, it's still inside you. The minute you get right with God, it comes to life again.

I once heard of a preacher who had a great healing anointing, but fell away from God. He was in a bar one night, half drunk, when someone had a heart attack. This backslidden preacher jumped down from his bar stool, repented quickly, laid his hands on the person and got him healed! After that, the backslidden preacher went back to drinking! It amazes me how the anointing keeps working through people.

Living What You Preach

We ministers preach well, but living what we preach is the problem. That's why we need to get in prayer lines and have other preachers pray for us while they are under the anointing. Sometimes we preachers need prayer to help with the problems in our natural lives.

It's not wrong for preachers to pray for one another. It helps. But pride will sometimes keep preachers from receiving prayer, even when they are fighting a physical ailment.

There was a time when I had problems with my jaws popping. I would be sitting in meetings when a word of knowledge would come regarding jaws, but I would just sit there, too embarrassed to go forward. I knew there was an anointing present to heal my jaws, but I struggled with the issue of prestige. I thought, "should I act like everything is fine, or should I go up there and get healed?" I finally said, "forget this," and I went up and got healed!

Letting Others Pray For You

When you're in the anointing, it's like you're on a high. Everything is great. You have no problems. You're ready to take on the world. But when the anointing lifts, you have to return to reality. You have to live from the Word and the strength of your inner man.

Pastors and ministers, there may come a time when someone in your church has an anointing to pray for you about a certain area. When it happens, you've got to acknowledge that it is from God and receive it.

I was holding some meetings in Missouri once, and as the pastor and I were heading for his office after the service, a lady came down the aisle and headed straight for me. I could tell that she wasn't interested in saying "hello." The anointing was on her.

As the ushers were about to turn her away, I said, "Hold it! She's okay!"

She marched right up, pointed her finger in my face, and laid a message in tongues on me! When she finished, she whirled around, marched back down the aisle, and left. She didn't even give me the interpretation.

The pastor said, "Do you want to leave?"

I said, "No. That was God. I'm going to wait here until I get the interpretation."

Suddenly, the pastor received a stirring and delivered the interpretation with the same intensity the woman had delivered the tongue. It was the Word of the Lord, and it was something I needed to know.

God was a little bit upset with me because I had been going in the wrong direction. He said, "Get back over there where you belong." The pastor had no idea what he was saying, but I sure did! Sometimes you say and do things you're not aware of when you're doing it by the Spirit.

5

A Call To Walk In The Spirit

I used to teach a lot on walking in the Spirit. Over the past few years I have not done a lot of that, and the Lord said to me, "You've got to keep preaching on life in the Spirit." Our success in life and ministry depends on how we live our life in the Spirit. We cannot war unless we live in the Spirit. We cannot have the right kind of relationships unless we live in the Spirit. We cannot survive in the last days unless we live in the Spirit. Jesus said, *"In the last days it will be like it was in the days of Noah."* (Mat. 24:37) God told Noah to build an ark of safety. It is a symbol of our salvation; it symbolizes our life in the Spirit. As the return of the Lord draws near, we need to be more aware of inward happenings than outward happenings. When something happens, we need to be able to turn inward and listen to what the Holy Spirit is saying. We need to be sensitive to Him, appreciate Him and draw upon Him. We need to let Him be our friend.

Life in the Spirit is a continuous relationship with the Trinity — the Father, the Son, and the Holy Spirit. It means we become Their friend, talking to Them, drawing upon Them, and leaning upon Them. We can't lean on our own understanding, because that aborts the flow of the Holy Spirit.

We need to be reminded of these things, because sometimes we assume we're doing them when we're not. When we realize our error, we can say, "I have missed it here, Lord. I'm not as strong as I used to be in this area. I need to develop this again."

Most of you have been led by the Spirit of God to accomplish what you have done so far. But for you to continue to succeed, you must continue to be led by the Spirit. As Paul wrote to the Galatians:

Are ye so foolish? having begun in the Spirit, are ye now made perfect by the flesh? (Galatians 3:3)

Are you made perfect by the flesh? No, you are made perfect by walking in the Spirit, doing the Word, and making the decision to be more aware of the spirit world than the natural world you live in.

You can walk in the natural, do what you have to do, be normal and natural, and still be strong, alert and aware in the Spirit.

Most ministers started their ministries by the Spirit. They started by prayer, intercession, preaching the bold, uncompromised Word of God, and moving in the gifts of the Spirit. All these things helped build their ministries. Are you still walking that way? Are you still willing to flow that way?

Growth does not mean you discard the things that helped make you what you are. Growth means you increase those things until you become stronger in them.

Are You Still Moving With God?

As ministries grow and prestige and challenges come, ministers may be tempted not to move like they did in the beginning days of their ministries.

So I would like to ask, "Do you still have an altar call at your church? Do you still have a prayer line at your church? Do you still move in the gifts of the Spirit? Do you still do the things you did before?

"Well, yes, Roberts." Then let me ask you another question: To what dimension?

Perhaps you move in them once in a while, but is there a consistent flow of the gifts in your life and ministry? Is this flow growing? Is it becoming stronger? If not, return to your prayer closet and begin to crave and desire those spiritual things again (1 Cor 14:1). Tell the Father, "I want these things in my life and ministry. I repent of not stepping out in faith and desiring them more, voicing them more, and ministering with them more. I'm sorry, Father, and from this day forth I'll flow in them more."

Tell Heaven you are willing to flow with everything the Word offers. Don't be picky over certain gifts. Don't say, "I like this gift better than that gift."

If you get too picky, my friend, you won't get any of them! Receive them all. Renew your commitment to flow again in the Spirit, only stronger this time.

If you will do this, pastors, your church will go into shock over what happened to you! You will be on fire as you preach. You will be moving in the gifts of the Spirit. When you get through, people will be shaking under the power and manifestations of the Spirit will be happening all over the sanctuary.

That's what we need today — a fresh move of the Holy Spirit! Moves of the Holy Spirit are not always dramatic, but there can be dramatics when they come. Don't be afraid when something dramatic happens. Some people have to have dramatics all the time. I like them myself. My attitude is, "Yes, let it roll! Let's go!" I refuse to lose this attitude.

People keep trying to tell me, "That's because you're young, Roberts." But when I get old, I still want to be like this! I don't want to lose it — I want to keep it — so don't try to take it away from me.

Quit trying to make me old and dried up. Let me be like Dr. Lester Sumrall, who was active in ministry to the end of his life, going everywhere. That's the way all believers should be.

Hold On To The Things From Heaven!

Just because you've grown older, and you know more than when you started doesn't mean you should stop moving in the Spirit. Hold onto the things that are from Heaven! Don't let them go. Pray, "Father, I want your spiritual gifts to grow and increase in my life."

Some of you husbands and wives once flowed in tongues and interpretation. Are you still flowing like that, or do you think you've grown to a place where you don't need to flow in the gifts anymore? You must do what the Holy Spirit wants. He may not require you to flow in the gifts all the time, but always be willing to flow.

Some will argue, "But Roberts, I flowed in the Spirit, but I came under attack, and I got hurt."

You must get over that hurt and fear. Remember, Jesus came to heal the brokenhearted and those who have been bruised (Luke 4:18). He came to put you back together again so you can be stronger and continue your walk with Him.

A sign of Christian maturity is how quickly you overcome problems. Don't camp around those hurts. If it takes you six months to a year to get over your hurts, you are in a "maintenance" type of ministry. You are going around in a little circle.

The thing that holds you in that circle — even though you desire to get out of it — is the fear that threatens, "If you do this, such-and-such will happen, if you do that, this other terrible thing will happen. You must overcome those fears.

Be like the apostle Paul. The whole city of Ephesus was in an uproar and the people wanted to kill him, but Paul said, "let me go preach to them!" He didn't let their rejection bother him. He didn't whimper and say, "This whole city doesn't like me! I guess I'd better check to see if I'm really called to the ministry."

No, Paul didn't question his call. He said, "Let me at them!" That's the way you need to be. Don't let your soul get offended. Watch what offends you, and if you sense an offense, take care of it and grow stronger in the Spirit.

Some of you need to learn how to flow more accurately in the Spirit. You drift in and out of the Spirit while you're ministering. You must learn how to stay in the Spirit. This is why spiritual relationships and associations are important.

Get Connected!

If you will cry out to Him, God will connect you with those who have stability in their lives and ministries. He will join you with people who have developed these attributes so you can learn how to develop them too.

It's time to know people by the Spirit. It's time to discern those whom God has ordained for you to be connected with. It's time to quit walking in the flesh and return to a life of walking in the Spirit!

BOOKS

by Roberts Liardon

A Call To Action

Cry Of The Spirit

Extremists, Radicals and Non-Conformists

Final Approach

Forget Not His Benefits

God's Generals

Haunted Houses, Ghosts, And Demons

Holding To The Word of The Lord

I Saw Heaven

Kathryn Kuhlman

Knowing People By The Spirit

On Her Knees

Religious Politics

Run To The Battle

School of The Spirit

Sharpening Your Discernment

Smith Wigglesworth - Complete Collection

Smith Wigglesworth Speaks To Students

Spiritual Timing

The Invading Force

The Most Dangerous Place To Be

The Price of Spiritual Power

The Quest For Spiritual Hunger

Three Outs and You're In

*To place an order call (949) 833-3555
or visit our website at: www.robertsliardon.org*

AUDIO TAPES *by Roberts Liardon*

Acts of The Holy Spirit
Be Strong In The Lord
Breaking the Cycle of Failure
Changing Spiritual Climates
God's Secret Agents
Haunted Houses, Ghosts, & Demons
How To Combat Demonic Forces
How To Stay On The Mountaintop
How To Stir Up Your Calling
    and Walk In Your Gifts
How To Survive An Attack
Increasing Your Spiritual Capacity
I Saw Heaven
Life & Ministry of Kathryn Kuhlman
Living On The Offensive
No More Religion
Obtaining Your Financial Harvest
Occupy 'Til He Comes
Personality of the Holy Spirit
Prayer 1 - How I Learned To Pray
Prayer 2 - Lost In The Spirit
Reformers & Revivalists
Rivers of Living Water (Grams)
School of The Spirit
Seven Steps of Demonic Posession
Sharpening Your Discernment (One)
Sharpening Your Discernment (Two)

Spirit Life
Spiritual Climates
Storms of His Presence
Taking A City
Tired? How To Live In The
    Divine Life of God
True Spiritual Strength
The Anointing
The Healing Evangelists
The Charges of St. Paul - 1 Timothy
The Charges of St. Paul - 2 Timothy
The Working of Miracles
    & Divine Health
Three Arenas of Authority
    & Conflict
Three Worlds: God, You,
    & The Devil
Tired? How To Live In The
    Divine Life Of God
Tongues And Their Diversities
True Spiritual Strength
Useable Faith
Victorious Living In The Last Days
Working The Word
What You Need To Keep
    Under To Go Over
Your Faith Stops The Devil

To place an order call (949) 833-3555
or visit our website at: www.robertsliardon.org

Spirit Life Partner

Wouldn't It Be Great...

- If you could feed over 1,000 hungry people every week?

- If you could travel 250,000 air miles, boldly preaching the Word of God in 93 nations?

- If you could strengthen and train the next generation of God's leaders?

Project Joseph Food Outreach.

- If you could translate 23 books and distribute them into 37 countries?

...Now You Can!

Maybe you can't go, but by supporting this ministry every month, your gift can help to communicate the gospel around the world.

------------------- CLIP ALONG LINE & MAIL TO ROBERTS LIARDON MINISTRIES. -------------------

☐ **YES!!** Pastor Roberts, I want to support your work in the kingdom of God by becoming a **SPIRIT LIFE PARTNER.** Please find enclosed my first monthly gift.

Name _____

Address _____

City _____ State _____ Zip _____

Phone (_____) _____

SPIRIT LIFE PARTNER AMOUNT: $ _____

☐ Check / Money Order   ☐ VISA   ☐ American Express   ☐ Discover   ☐ MasterCard

☐☐☐☐ ☐☐☐☐ ☐☐☐☐ ☐☐☐☐

Name On Card_____ Exp. Date___/___/___

Signature_____ Date___/___/___

Roberts Liardon Ministries

P.O. Box 30710 ♦ Laguna Hills, CA 92654 ♦ (949) 833-3555 ♦ Fax (949) 833.9555 ♦ www.robertsliardon.org

VIDEO TAPES *by Roberts Liardon*

2+2=4

And The Cloud Came

A New Generation

Apostles, Prophets
    & Territorial Churches

Apostolic Alignment

Are You A Prophet?

Confronting The Brazen Heavens

Developing An Excellent Spirit

Don't Break Rank

Does Your Pastor Carry A Knife?

Forget Not His Benefits

God's Explosive Weapons

How To Be An End Time Servant

How To Be Healed
    of Spiritual Blindness

I Saw Heaven

Ministering To The Lord

No More Walls

Reformers And Revivalists (5 Vol.)

Spirit of Evangelism

The Importance of Praying
    In Tongues

The Lord Is A Warrior

The Most Dangerous Place To Be

The New Millennium Roar

The Operation of Exhortation

The Word of The Lord Came
    Unto Me Saying

True And False Manifestations

Was Jesus Religious?

Why God Wrote Verse 28

New God's Generals Video Collection

Volume 1 - John Alexander Dowie

Volume 2 - Maria Woodworth-Etter

Volume 3 - Evan Roberts

Volume 4 - Charles F. Parham &
    William J. Seymour

Volume 5 - John G. Lake

Volume 6 - Smith Wigglesworth

Volume 7 - Aimee Semple
    McPherson

Volume 8 - William Branham

Volume 9 - Jack Coe

Volume 10 - A. A. Allen

Volume 11 - Kathryn Kuhlman

Volume 12 - Highlights
    & Live Footage

Videos by Gladoylene Moore (Grams)

Foundations of Stone

God of the Breakthrough

How I Learned To Pray

How To Avoid Disaster

Seeking God

The Prophetic Flow

The Sword Of Gideon

The Warrior Names of God

To place an order call (949) 833-3555
or visit our website at: www.robertsliardon.org

Seven reasons you should attend Spirit Life Bible College

1. SLBC is a **spiritual school** with an academic support; not an academic school with a spiritual touch.

2. SLBC teachers are **successful ministers** in their own right. Pastor Roberts Liardon will not allow failure to be imparted into his students.

3. SLBC is a member of **Oral Roberts University Educational Fellowship** and is **fully accredited** by the International Christian Accreditation Association.

4. SLBC hosts monthly seminars with some of the **world's greatest** ministers who add another element, anointing and impartation to the students' lives.

5. Roberts Liardon understands your commitment to come to SLBC and commits himself to students by **ministering weekly** in classroom settings.

6. SLBC provides **hands-on** ministerial training.

7. SLBC provides ministry opportunity through its **post-graduate placement program**.

---------------------- CLIP ALONG LINE & MAIL TO ROBERTS LIARDON MINISTRIES. ----------------------

☐ **YES!!** Pastor Roberts, I am interested in attending **SPIRIT LIFE BIBLE COLLEGE**. Please send me an information packet.

Name _____

Address _____

City_____ State _____ Zip _____

Phone (_____) _____

Roberts Liardon Ministries
P.O. Box 30710 ♦ Laguna Hills, CA 92654
(949) 833-3555 ♦ Fax (949) 833.9555
www.robertsliardon.org

ROBERTS LIARDON MINISTRIES
INTERNATIONAL OFFICES

EUROPE
Roberts Liardon Ministries
P.O. Box 295
Welwyn Garden City
AL7 2ZG
England
011-44-1707-327-222

SOUTH AFRICA
Roberts Liardon Ministries
P.O. Box 3155
Kimberely 8300
South Africa
011-27-53-832-1207

AUSTRALIA
Roberts Liardon Ministries
P.O. Box 1076
Buderim, Qld 4556
Australia
011-61-500-555-056

Roberts Liardon Ministries
P.O. Box 30710
Laguna Hills, California, USA
92654-0710
Telephone: (949) 833-3555
Fax: (949) 833-9555
Visit our website at: www.robertsliardon.org